A note from the author: We have all heard someone say, "The devil made me do it." But what if he took a siesta? This story is not so much about the devil, but about one's behavior in his absence.

Published by Paloma Press, Santa Fe, New Mexico. First edition limited to 2,500. Design: Maria Levy. Production: Swell Design, Inc.

Printed in China.

ISBN: 0-9719364-0-4

SIESTA

(sē es′tə) *n.* A brief nap or rest after the noon meal.

BY JOEL NAKAMURA

PALOMA PRESS *Santa Fe, New Mexico*

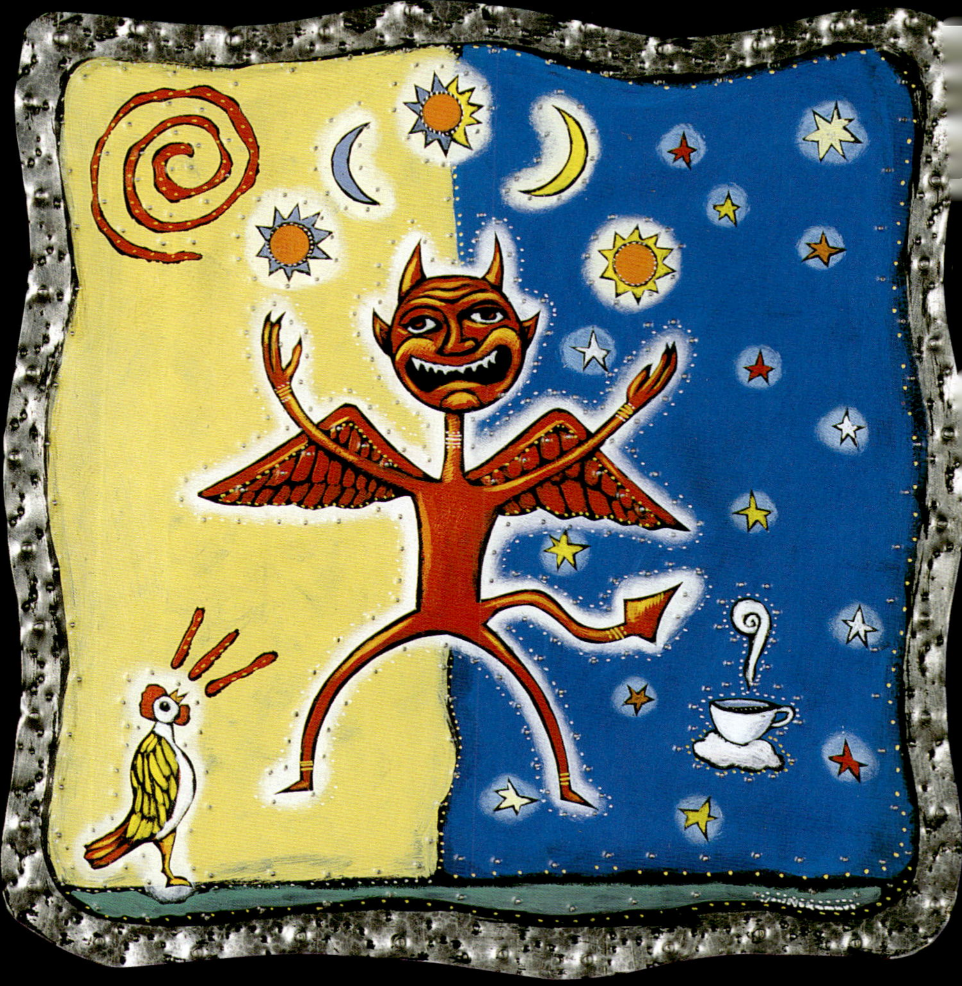

Day and night,
juggling mischief and coffee,
I would sure like a
siesta!

I assume many **personalities.**
I wear many **disguises.**

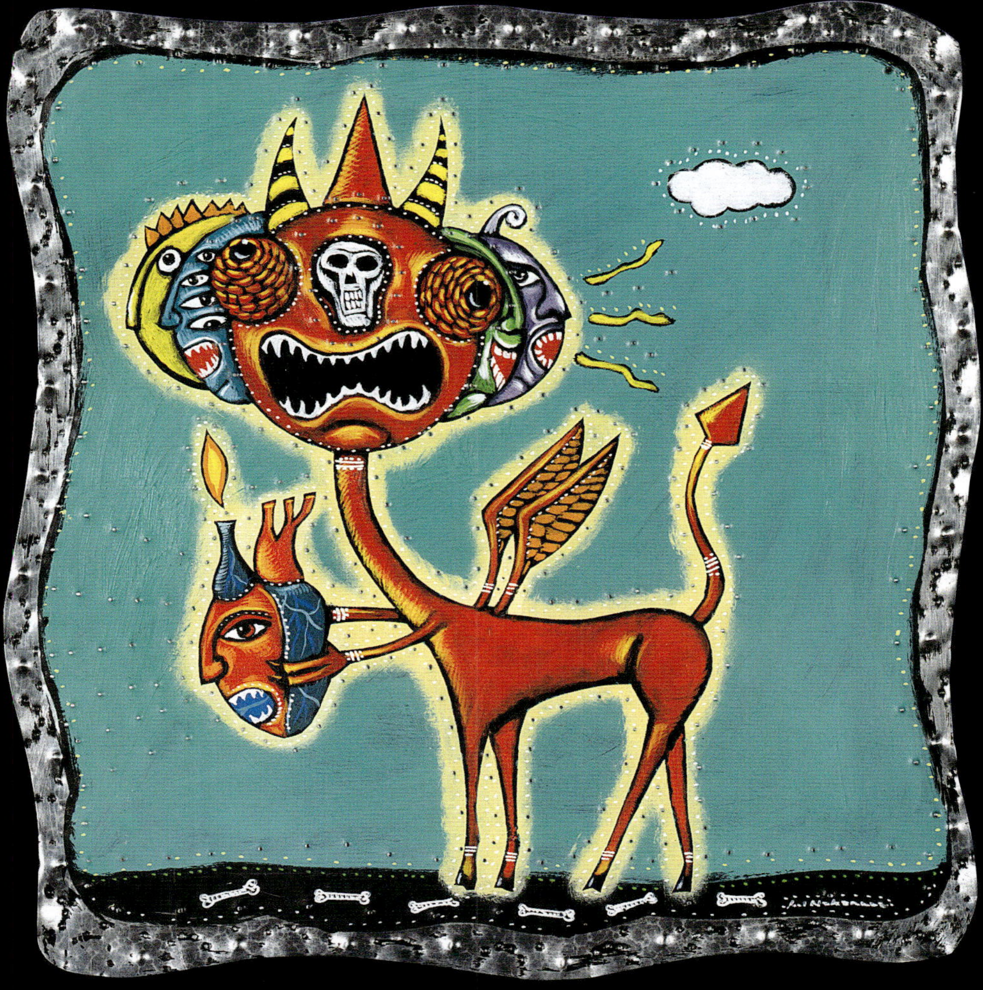

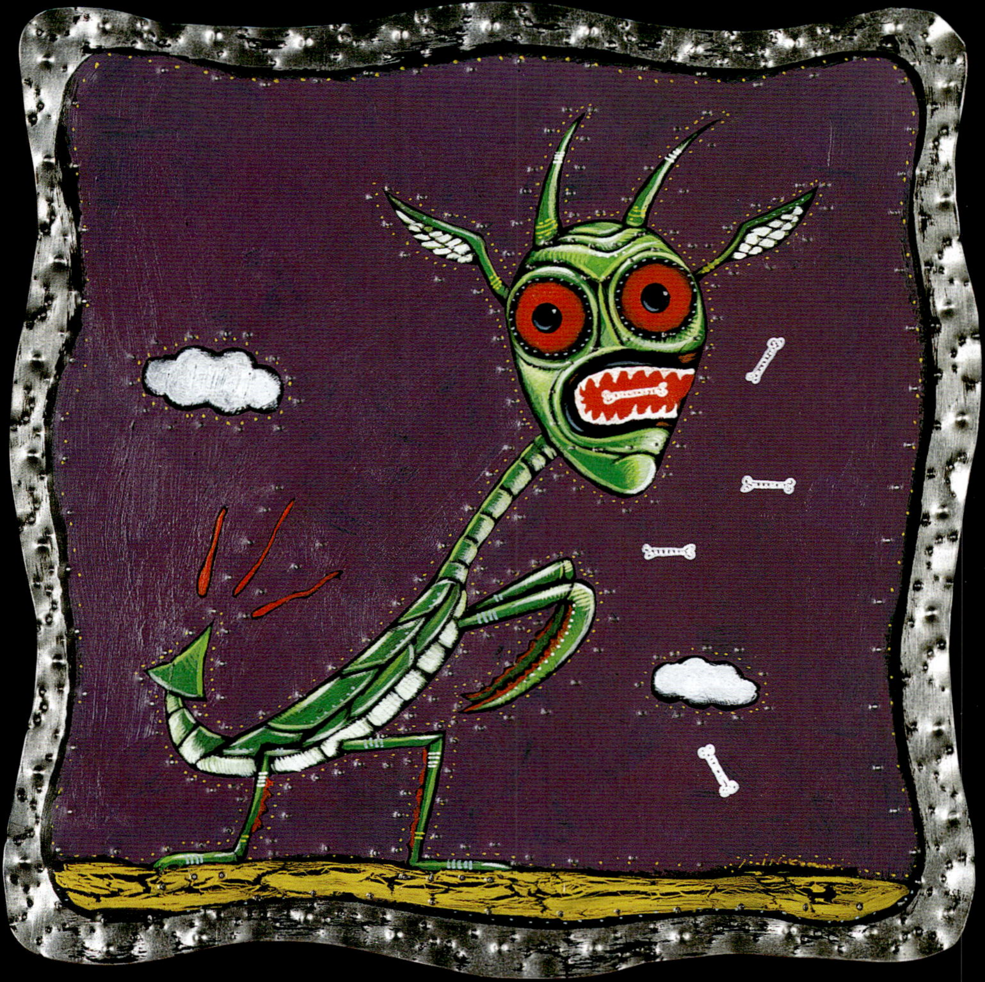

Sometimes I am **GREEN.**

Sometimes I am **BLUE.**

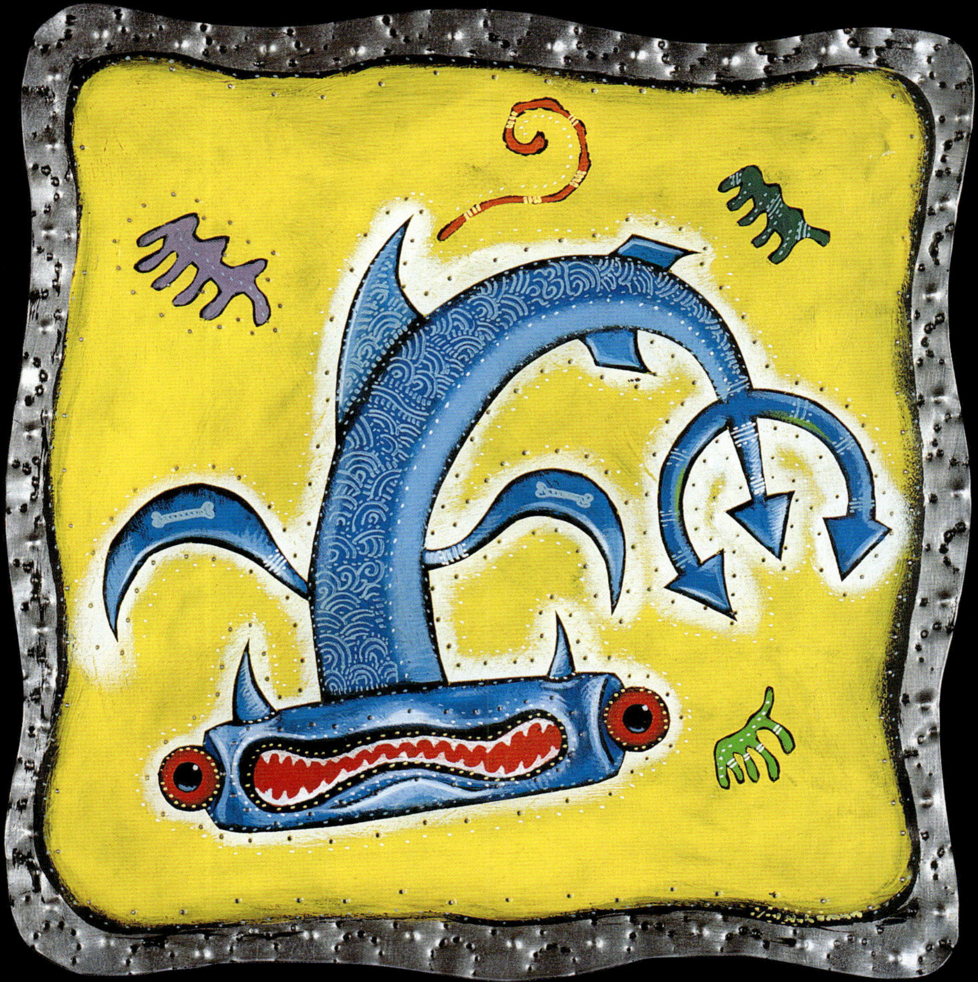

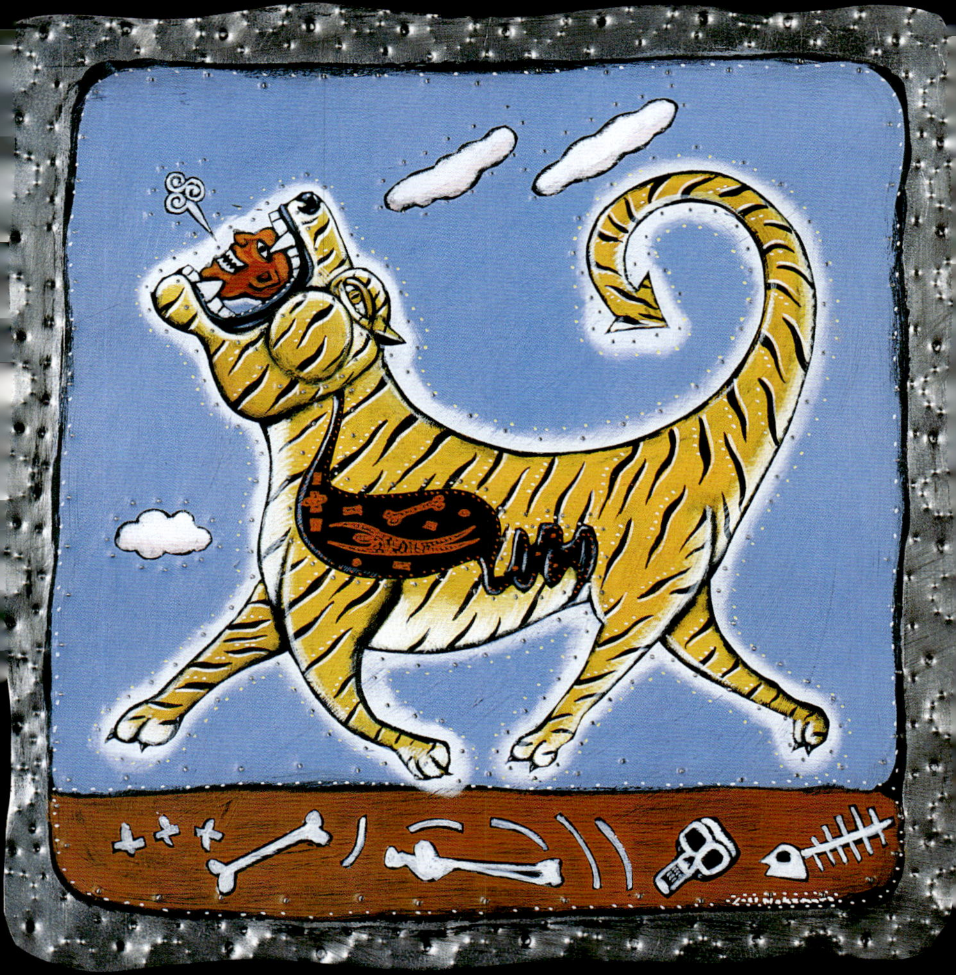

I am rather fond of wearing STRIPES.

Sometimes I WHISPER . . .

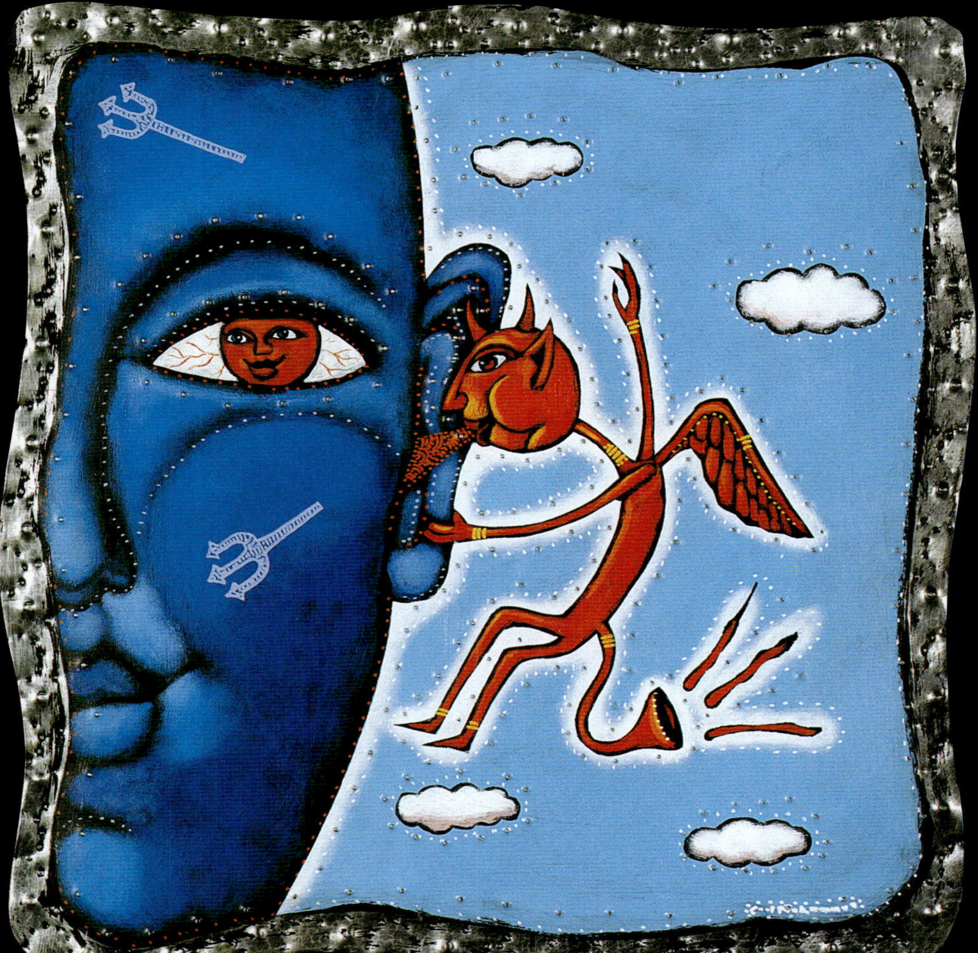

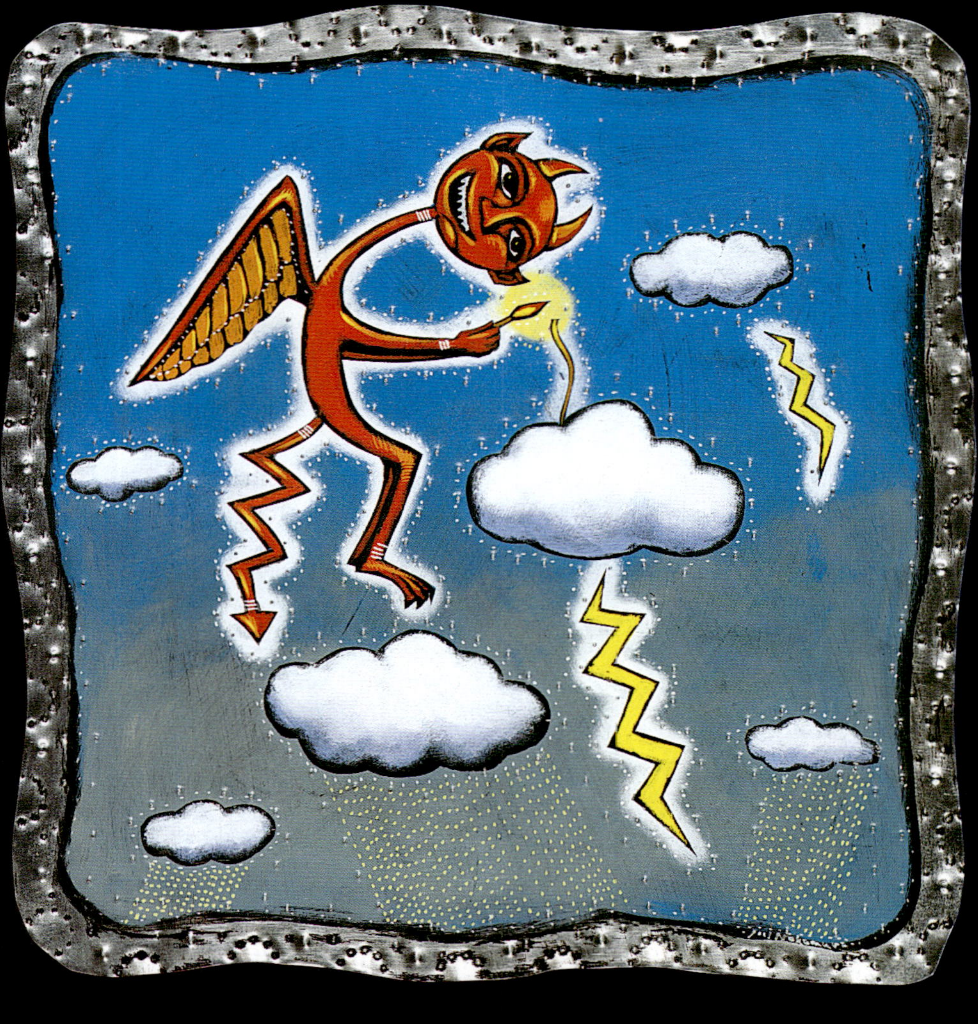

Sometimes I am very loud.

CRACK!

My favorite game is called

STRETCH THE SOUL.

My brother usually wins.

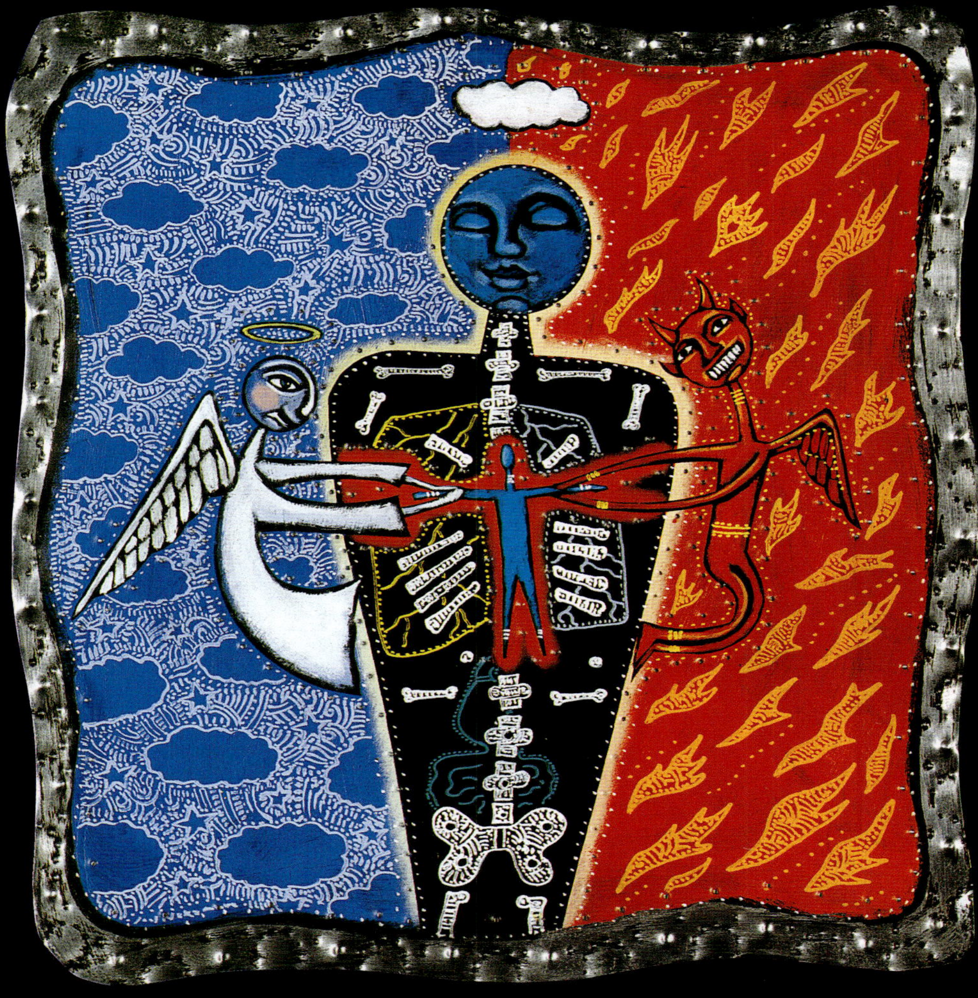

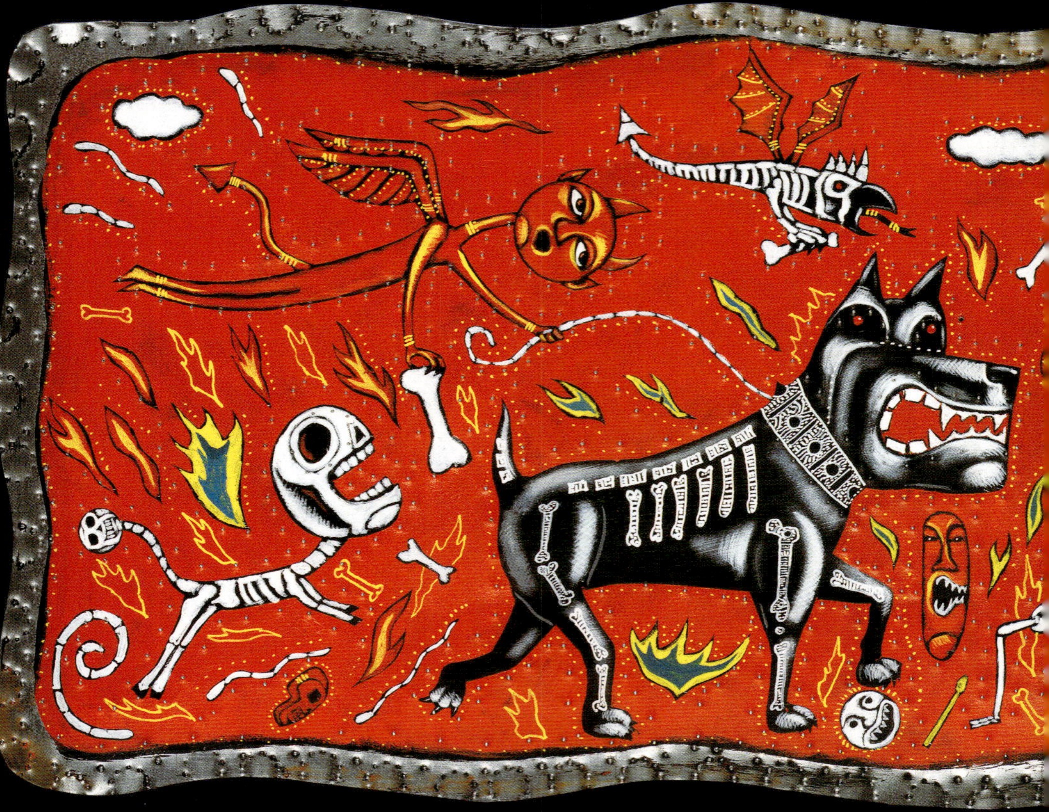

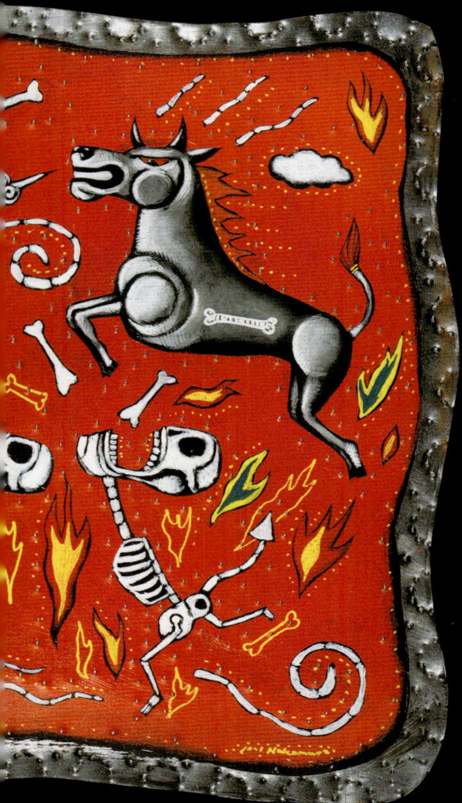

I stoke the fire.
I walk the skeletons.

I am

the superduper
pooper scooper.

I am really tired. What time is it?

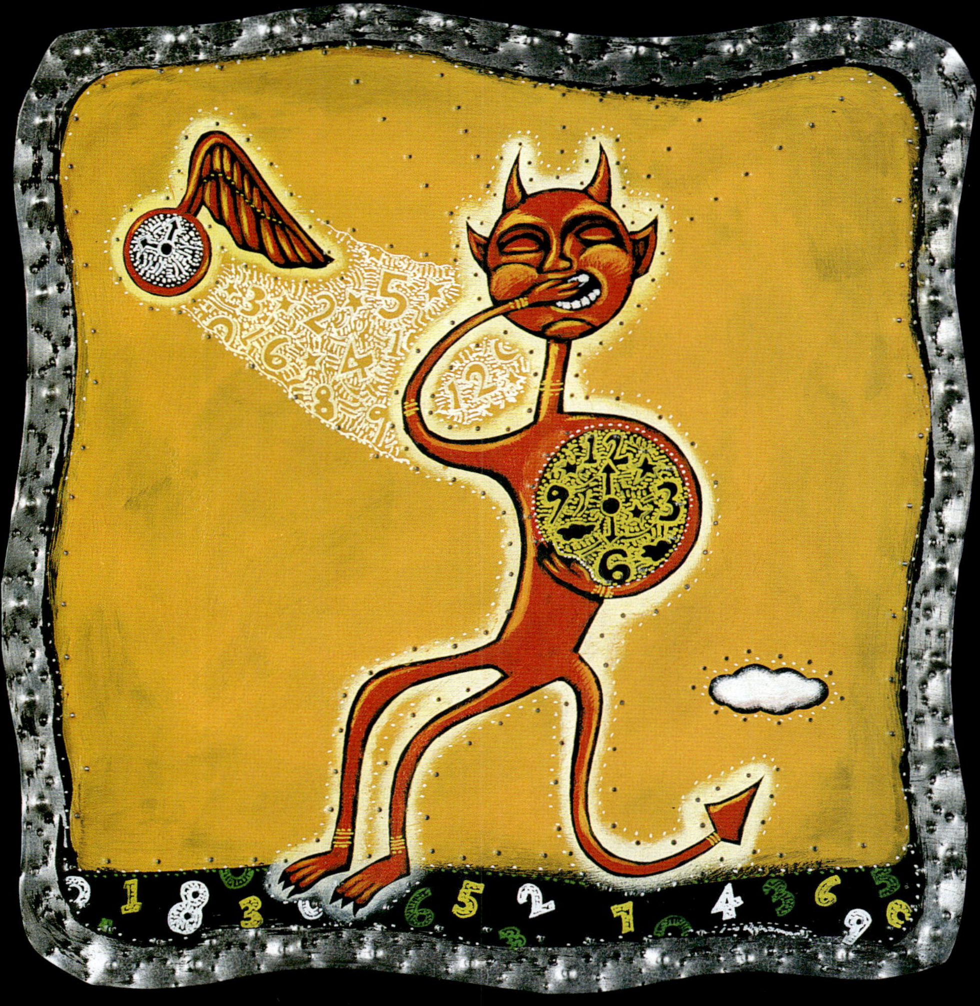

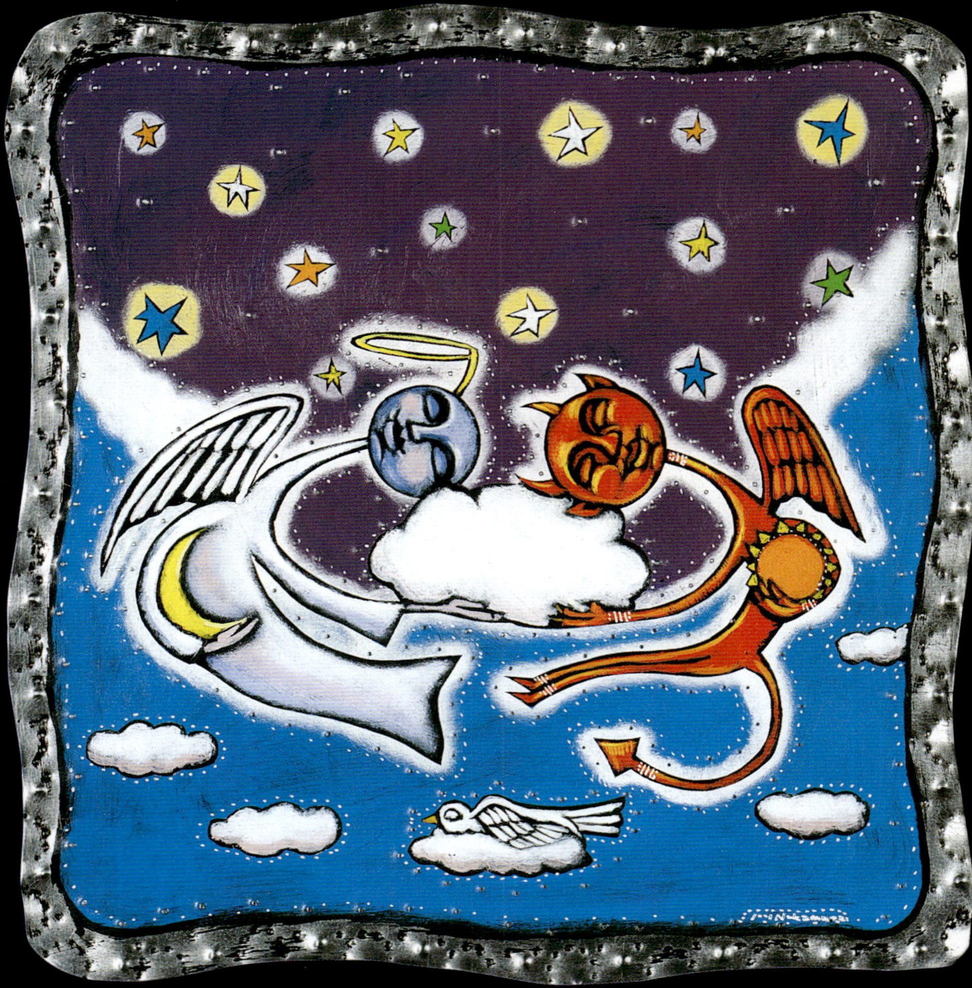

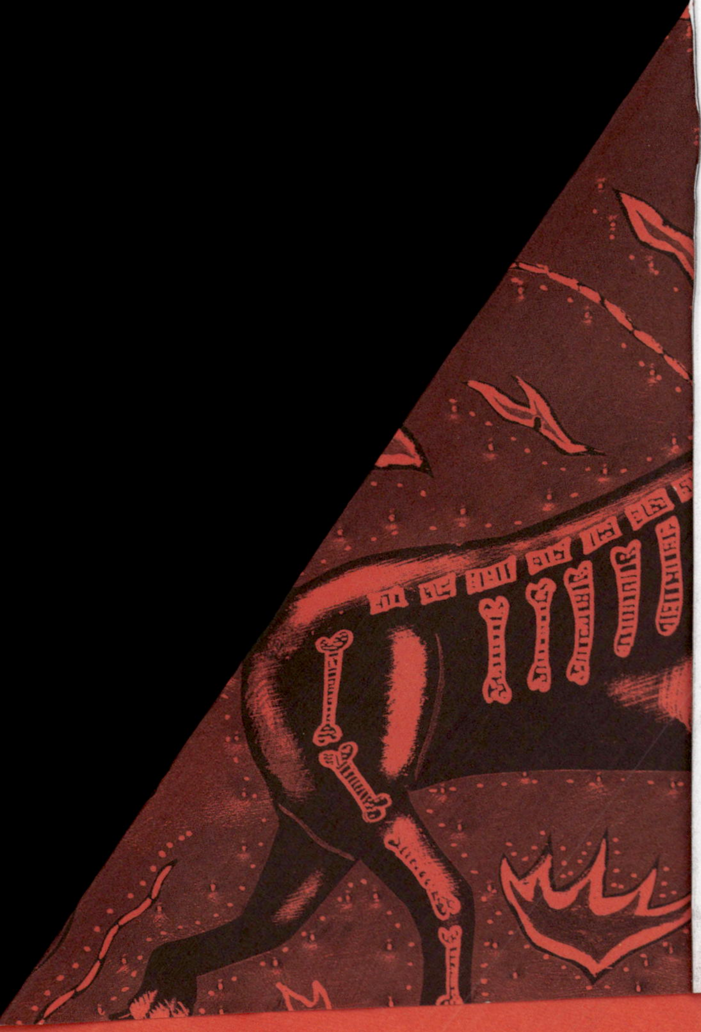

Ah! I finally get my

siesta!

What mischief happens
in the world right now
is up to you.

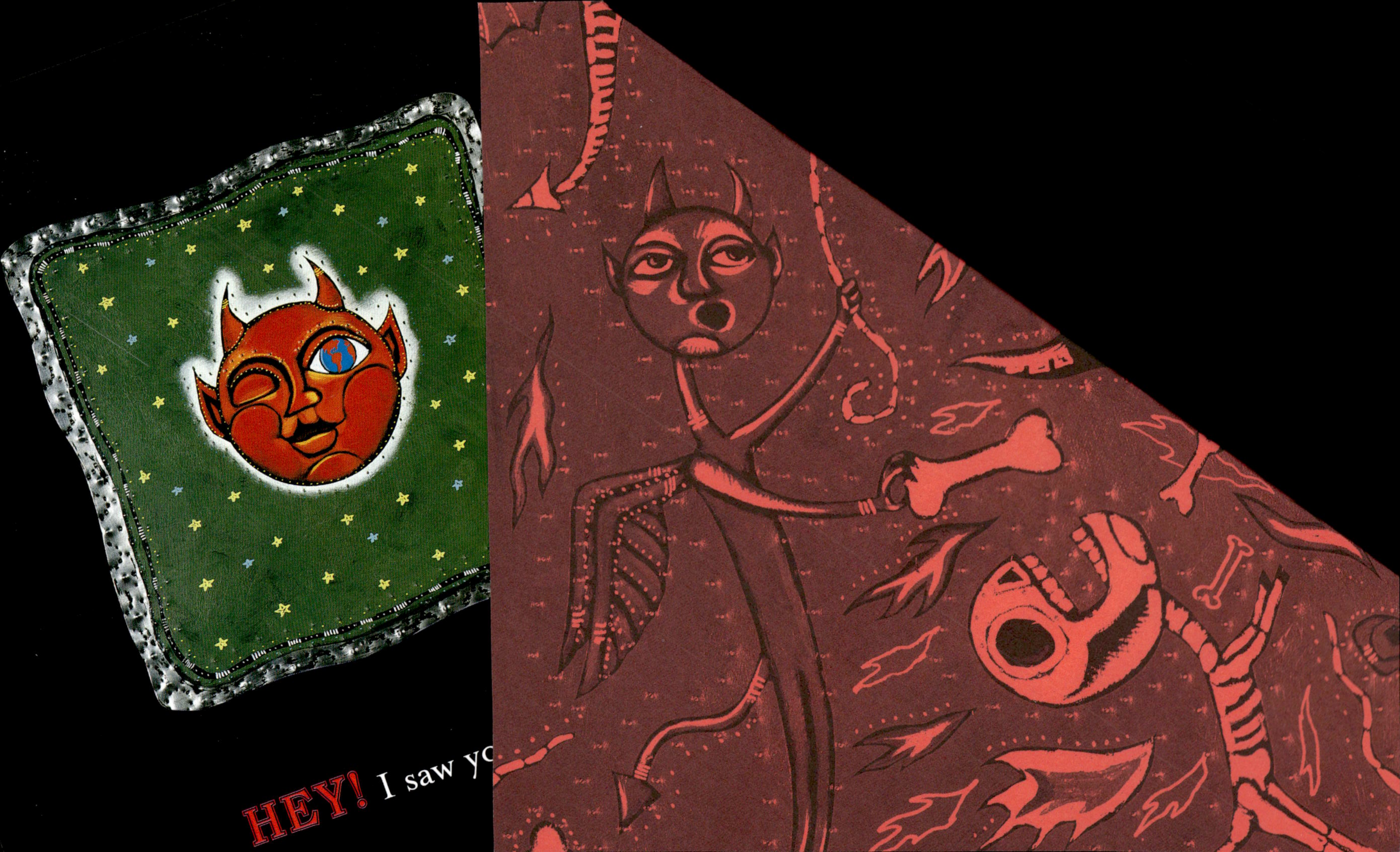
HEY! I saw yo

Ah! I finally get my

siesta!

What mischief happens
in the world right now
is up to you.

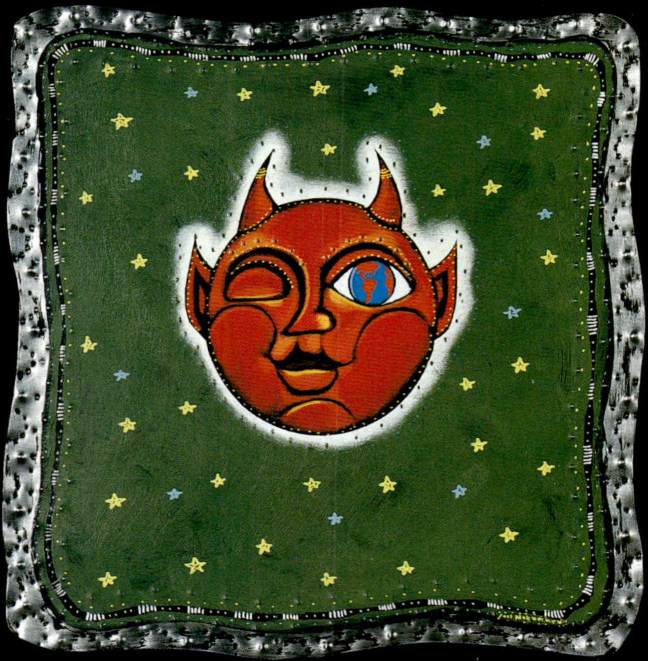

HEY! I saw you do that!

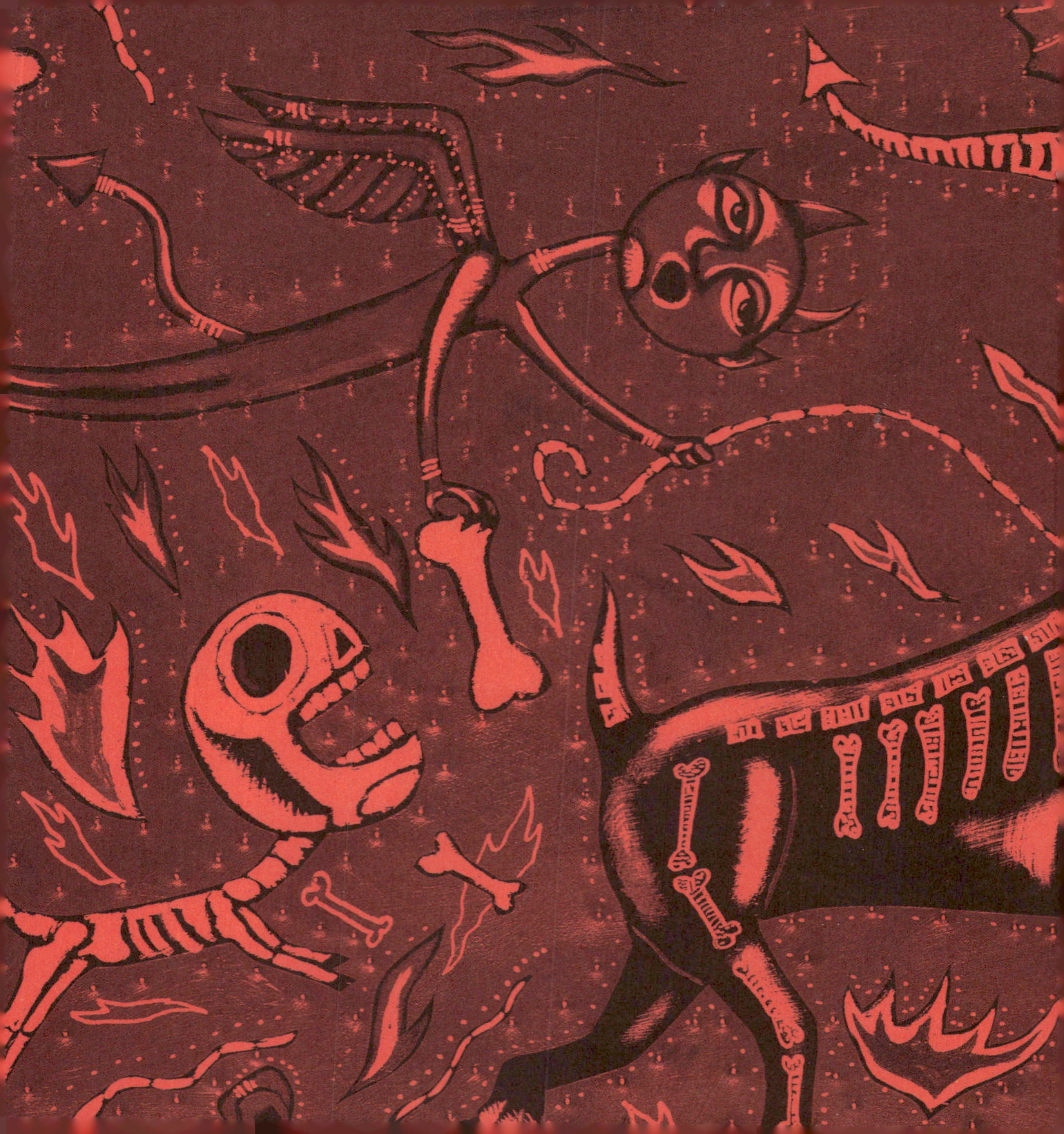